# A Journey to
## The Billy ___ ___

### From a life of violence to a life of grace

Published in 2018

Copyright @2018

# Dedication

To the God of Heaven; every time I think about my
story, I just cannot help but give You the glory. Thank
you, Lord, for Your grace and mercy.

To my mother, Kadene Oakley, who never gave up on
me. Mommy, without your prayers and unconditional
love, my life would, be a dark night that has no day.

To the love of my life, Abigail. Thank you for believing
in me when I doubted myself.
You are more than my wife; you are my inspiration.

# Contents

# Foreword

I first met Billy on Facebook where we became friends. Since then I've followed him and took careful note of the apparent demand for him to share his life experience in churches and social gatherings.

Being curious about hearing more of his seemingly stunning life experience, I invited him to share at one of our morning worship sessions at the General Conference Inter-American Division on May 23, 2017. What an experience it was! There was not an eye that remained dry in that auditorium when we ended the session.

How could a young man, in fact, a child, become so caught up in the dark side of life? In a tunnel to nowhere! Is there anyone who questions the reality of demon possession? Do you know the extent to which persons can be innocently swallowed up or engulfed by demon possession?

How about God's grace? Have you experienced it or seen it at work in the life of a wayward, self-centered child or youth bent on destroying others unmindful of the personal impact and consequences? It is truly amazing how God can transform sinners and have them transition course and be able to tell their stories. Grace is indeed marvelous!

# Foreword

The story of Billy Mirander's life outlined in these pages highlights both sides; the side of darkness and demon possession and the side of grace and transformation. Children will find it instructive, young people will discover it relevant, adults will be awed and parents will be informed.

Just read it!

Dr. Balvin B. Braham
Administrative Field Secretary
Assistant to the President for Evangelism and Leadership Development
Chair, Growth and Consolidation Strategic Planning Committee
General Conference Inter-American Division

# Introduction

Were it not for grace that afforded me a U-turn while I was driving down the road of No Returns, it is highly likely that you would have met me in the obituary section of the newspaper. The God of Heaven revealed Himself to me through a series of experiences that changed the direction of my life, from the dark tunnel to nowhere to this completely new highway, destined to paradise.

Fifty percent of boys in Jamaica are 11 times more likely to display violent behavior; nine times more likely to run away from home and become crime victims or perpetrators of crime; twice as likely to drop out of school; nine times more likely to become gang members; and six times more likely to end up in prison, according to Dr Michael Coombs, founder of the National Association of the Family. His findings are based on research done in the United States, United Kingdom and the Caribbean. The

# Introduction

study concludes that fatherless children may be one of the primary reasons for the crime epidemic.

Gang life appears glamourous to some young men, since it is laced with the strappings of fame, power, women, and money. Yet, the time-tested biblical truth chronicled in Proverbs 14:12, KJV, points out that, There is a way which seemeth right unto a man, but the end thereof are the ways of death." Quite often the road that glistens results in a reserved spot at the nearest cemetery or accommodations at the penitentiary.

If you've made decisions that you regret, done things you would prefer to forget, or wished that you could live your life over again, then I invite you to journey with me as I unfold the dark tunnels through which my life has passed. Then you'll understand how amazing the U-turn was that God granted me which forever changed the direction of my life.

# Chapter 1

## Birth and Early Days

The day was October 18, 1993, when the great clock of time announced the birth of a bouncing baby boy, weighing 10 pounds. I made my debut into the world at the Spanish Town Hospital in St. Catherine, Jamaica. It was a moment of sheer ecstasy and joy for my proud parents, Kadene Oakley and Allairus Mirander. My mother and father were together from their teenage years until I reached kindergarten; however, their relationship became filled with tension and came to an abrupt end not long after.

I grew up in a large family home in the community of Sharper Lane, Old Harbour, Jamaica with my grandmother, aunties, uncle, siblings, and other relatives. I was deeply loved by my grandmother, Ruby Oakley, who worked as a hairdresser and dressmaker in the community. I received part

# Birth and Early Days

of my early training from Grandma, with whom I shared a tight bond. To provide for my siblings and me, my mother accepted a job as a bartender in Kingston, Jamaica. Bars operate very late into the night, which resulted in her coming home in the wee hours of the morning. One night the bar was robbed, during which the robbers accosted my mother, ripping both of her banged earrings from her ears leaving a tear in each ear lobe. When the bar manager arrived, his primary concern was how much money was taken. My mother took note of this and decided to change her occupation by starting a clothing business, selling clothes from door to door. This allowed her to take care of our needs and spend more time with my siblings and me.

My early education began in the parish of St. Catherine, Jamaica. I started kindergarten in September 1996 to June 1999 at the Old Harbour Seventh-day Adventist Basic School.

# Birth and Early Days

Thereafter, from September 1999 to June 2005, I attended Old Harbour Primary School. In kindergarten my teacher, Mrs. Edgar, described me as a very peaceful, calm and diligent student. She mentioned that on some days I would sit and day dream for short periods of time; but once she called to me, I would quickly direct my attention to the lesson at hand. In primary school, it was clear that I wanted to excel. I was a very helpful to my teachers; but there were several underlying issues that affected my ability to perform at my best.

From a very tender age I loved hanging around men and women who were much older than me. Their line of conversation was always interesting and I learned a lot from them. As a result, I matured mentally a lot faster than my age. Aside from the girlfriend I had in second grade, and other young girls that I admired, I recognized that I had a greater admiration and interest in older ladies.

# Birth and Early Days

In third grade I developed a deep attraction for my teacher. She was fresh out of university, and I liked her very much. I showed my interest in her by complimenting her on the beauty of her face and the contours of her shape, but she didn't respond to me the same way. One day she instructed me to read a section of a book. However, since she hadn't responded favorably to me I felt she didn't like me, so I refused to comply with her instructions. She gave me a beating, after which I told her that I would make my "gangster friend, shoot her."

In those days my stepfather, Everton Blender – a popular singer in Jamaica – and my mother, who took care of several community children, were well-respected. Even though I was surrounded by many "gangsters" in my community, at no time did I get involved with them or have the slightest intention of using these connections.

My teacher reported the incident to the principal who gave me a second dose of corporal punishment and sent me home. The next morning on my way to school, a police car pulled up in front of me; little did I know that my teacher's husband was a police officer. The teacher jumped out of the car brandishing a pair of handcuffs and a gun.

"These are real handcuffs and real gun, and I know how to use them; so you need to leave me alone," she made no bones about telling me.

Taken aback, by her actions, the flame of attraction in my heart for my teacher dwindled. The crushing reality hit me like a bolt of lightning; a relationship with her would never be a reality, now or ever.

In sixth grade, I found myself deeply attracted to my teacher, again. I thought she was very beautiful, pleasant, and just an all-around nice woman. Because I did very well in mathematics, science and social studies, she repeatedly called on me to show the other students how to arrive at the answers – especially in math, as that was my best subject. The teacher also often commented on my attire, motivating me to look my best every day. After some time, her warm greetings to me, her compliments of me, and the special attention I received when she invited me to the board, led me to believe that she had "special feelings" for me.

One day in class after I completed a math worksheet and turned it in, the teacher called me and showed me that I'd gotten an answer incorrect. She gave me the opportunity to correct it since I was the first student to complete the worksheet. After returning to my seat and correcting my answer, I thought the time was right to put in my "letter of application," or love letter, to express my feelings to her, since − in my mind − the feelings were mutual.

When I turned in my corrected worksheet, I handed her my "letter of application" as well, and asked her to read it to the class. The letter said, "Miss, please meet me around the school back, and I will give you $JA200 (equivalent to $1.49 in

US dollars)." The class erupted in laughter, and immediately the guidance counselor was summoned to the classroom where she heard a report about my behavior. She gave me a dose of corporal punishment while saying, "You love too much big woman." Big woman in the Jamaica context refers to a woman that is senior in age to me.

As a part of my punishment, and with much protesting on my part, I was switched to a class with an older teacher, who didn't hesitate to use corporal punishment on me when needed. I had no choice but to settle down and pay more attention to my school work.

The Grade Six Assessment Test (GSAT) is a placement exam in Jamaica that is used for assigning students to secondary or high schools. These secondary or high schools are graded as traditional and non-traditional. The traditional schools are considered more reputable than the non-traditional schools, though the non-traditional ones were upgraded to High School status in more recent times. Students know the

## Birth and Early Days

significance of which schools they are placed in based on test

results. Parents are also anxious about this.

   I successfully passed the GSAT and was placed at the

Old Harbour High School, in St. Catherine, Jamaica. This was

my first choice. Though it was a non-traditional high school, it

was highly ranked among the schools in the country.

# Chapter 2

## Two deaths and the Pathway to Revenge

My grandmother's last child, Maria Celestine Forte, was a very beautiful and ambitious young lady. During high school she met a young man who, she thought, deeply loved 3.her. In a short time, their relationship produced two girls and a boy. Unfortunately, Maria's "Mr. Knight in Shining Amour," was an obsessive, jealous, and abusive man. If they were walking together and he thought another man looked at her, he beat her. If another man sent a text to her phone, he beat her.

Repeatedly my grandmother said to Auntie Maria, "Mar, if you do not leave this man, he is going to kill you."

My inexperienced aunt, who had a wrong conception of love, responded to her mother, saying, "It's because he loves me why he always beats me."

In December 2003, my grandmother was diagnosed with kidney problems, and later discovered that she also had cancer. She struggled for six to eight months, in and out of the hospital. Before she went back to the hospital, for what would be the last time, she called all of us – her children and grandchildren – to her bedside and bid each of us goodbye. Her parting words to my Auntie Maria were, "Mar, you have to leave this guy, or he is going to kill you."    Just a pause in the narrative: Young ladies, there are some things that your mother will see that you will not. Unfortunately for those who don't listen to wisdom, when they finally see, it's too late.

I was deeply endeared to my grandmother, as a considerable amount of my early days were spent at her feet learning the lessons of life. When she passed away, a part of my heart fell apart. This was the first time I had lost someone so dear and near to me. Grandma was that glue that kept our

# Two deaths and the Pathway to Revenge

family together. When she passed, the family became disjointed, each person going his or her own way. In 2005, Auntie Maria mustered up the courage to end the relationship with her children's father. She went to live in Barton's in St. Catherine, Jamaica. However, her children's father refused to accept her decision, stating, "If I can't have her back, no one else will get her." In a bid to force her back into the relationship, he refused to financially support the children and Auntie took him to court. Even so, Auntie Maria was very resourceful and ambitious, working in Old Harbour Town to provide for her three children as best as possible. Each evening after track and field training at Old Harbour High School, I would go by the Wholesale Supermarket in Gateway Plaza, Old Harbour where she worked, and escort her to the taxi stand to ensure her safety. After a period of heavy rain in October, Big Pond, a river which sandwiched the main roadway, became impassable.

# Two deaths and the Pathway to Revenge

In order to be in walking distance to her job, Auntie Maria went to stay with a relative in Claremont Heights in St. Catherine, Jamaica. After school I would still meet her after work and walk with her to Burke Road as she made her way home. On November 3, 2005, as was my usual practice, I went to the Wholesale Supermarket to accompany my aunt to Burke Road. However, that night she had to work late fine tuning some paperwork for the store, as its supervisor, so she told me that she'd be OK and to go on home.

Once I arrived home, my siblings and I decided to go shopping. As we passed by the shop on our way back home, we heard the earth-shattering news; Auntie Maria had been shot to death. We rushed to Burke Road and found that the police had already sectioned off the crime scene with those yellow strips. On the ground lay Auntie Maria. She had been shot twice; once in the head and once in the back. She was pronounced dead on the spot. When my mother arrived at the crime scene, she fainted at the sight of her sister on the ground. Neither I nor my other family members could hold back the liquid frustration that flowed uncontrollably from our eyes.

It wasn't long before my family was told that the father of my aunt's children had paid to have her killed. Earlier that week they had gone to court, at which time he had reportedly said, "This will be the final time that we come to court." He made good on his promise. This information gripped my heart, especially went I looked at my three young cousins facing life without a mother. It was more than my heart could take, and I purposed to exact revenge. My mind was resolute; the killers would not get away with what they did to my Aunty.

At the time of my aunt's death I was 12 years old. For one year and six months, vengeful thoughts grew in my mind and I became incensed with anger that I could no longer contain.

# Chapter 3
## Gangster Life Outside of School

Overcome with grief and a thirst for revenge, I made it my goal to join a gang to avenge my aunt's death. My journey into gang life was based on two premises: first, to take out the man who paid for my aunt's killing; and second, to take out the man who pulled the trigger. To accomplish this mission I needed to get some gangster friends and access to a firearm.

Although I wasn't certain whether or not I could find who and what I needed, I commenced preparing for war. While in high school, on numerous occasions I went to Kingston, the capital and largest city in Jamaica. I rode the bus to my Godmother's house, Auntie Juliet, who lived in that city. I would also frequently spend holidays, and some weekends, with her family.

# Gangster Life Outside of School

During the summer holiday of 2007, while visiting Auntie Juliet, my Godfather, Shawn Carr, took me to karate class. He was a black belt in karate, and also a member of the Jamaica Defense Force/ Military. There was a Boxing Gym nearby and I learned how to box, and – for the first time – I held a firearm.

Back in St. Catherine, Jamaica, I met a young man named TG, who is now deceased. When I told TG about my auntie's murder and my need to acquire a firearm to avenge her death, he told me that he was a part of a notorious gang. The members of this gang are blood tasters, which is a sign of viciousness and deadliness. TG said that if I won the trust of the "Don," – the gang leader – I could obtain my personal firearm.

In 2007, at the tender age of 13, with no time to lose, I worked assiduously to win the confidence of the older gang members so that I could gain access to a firearm and ultimately

# Gangster Life Outside of School

take out the man who abused my aunt, and her killer. Some of the things that I was required to do included looting, defeating their enemies, and performing any instructions that the "Don" gave. Suffice it to say that I successfully won the Don's confidence and was accepted into the gang, which afforded me my heart's desire. Gang membership placed me on a path of dense darkness.

At 14 years old – with no father or positive father figure to influence my life, and yearning for a father's presence – the gang offered me a place to belong. It also offered a way to quench my thirst for revenge. While in the gang, I engaged in some dreadful activities, including handling firearms, smoking, gambling, collecting extortion funds, and watching the Don's turf – territory – throughout the night. If an enemy trespassed, he would be eliminated. I watched the gang turf from 9 p.m. to 4 or 5 a.m., then I went to school at 7 a.m. The activities with gang took place each evening after school hours.

# Gangster Life Outside of School

During my time in the gang, I faced death several times. Here's one of those experiences: In those days in Jamaica, there was a special group of police officers termed the Death Squad. They were tasked with the responsibility of dismantling gangs. The Death Squad had determined that time had measured out the days of the gang that I belonged to. When the great clock of time pointed to the set hour, the Squad members used the darkness of the night to disguise their advance on the gang. Once the gang's hiding place had been successfully marked, the Squad glided like snakes, on their stomachs, in order to catch its prey without being detected.

That evening my mother somehow felt that something terrible was going to happen to me, and she – along with one of my older sisters – searched for me. Through searching and inquiring, my mother located the house where the gang stayed. One of the gang members came to the area of thick, tall shrubs where I was smoking and reasoning with some of the other gang members, and called me out. When I exited the shrubs and went to the house, I saw my mother, who was most upset with me. My Don intervened to calm her down, and encouraged her to go inside the house. I followed behind her, since dinner was being cooked and I had not eaten.

Just then, like the walls of Jericho in Bible times, the house was encompassed by the Death Squad. The officer at the front of the house opened fire, hitting the Don and his brother; both died on the spot. The Don's women, who were there, ran all over the place in the frenzy of flying bullets. My first thought was to run through the back door, but an officer armed with a M16 rifle stood there. My second thought was to jump through the window, but another officer with a rifle was looking at me, dead in the face. From the front door, an officer moved towards me with a Glock 40, the light from his gun aimed directly at me. As he drew nearer, I felt that my time to die had come. I could see the smoke rising from the muzzle; I was cornered without an escape route. I was sure I was facing my final moments.

As the police officer drew too near for comfort, my mother urinated on herself. Certain that her only son, at that time, was about to be killed, she poured out the anguish of her soul to God through tears, whispering prayers for mercy. As my mother held my hand, the officer commanded her to step away from me. Tremblingly, she let my hand go and death seemed more near than ever. The officer stepped back then came forward, about to squeeze the trigger, but stopped his arm in mid-air. He stepped back again, then came forward, about to squeeze the trigger and blow out my brains. I braced for the "Pow" signaling my death. Yet, in mid-air he stopped again.

An officer standing nearby said, "Aren't you going to take him out?"

The officer turned to me, and said, "I'm going to kill you this time."

# Gangster Life Outside of School

He stepped back for the last time and launched his body forward, his hand on the trigger. Staring me down he said, "Say your prayers."

I knew this was it; but again, he stopped in mid-air. By this time, the noise from the prior shooting had alerted the community, and a host of residents came to the house. As they surveyed the dead bodies littering the ground outside, their blood-curdling cries pierced the darkness, driving the officers quickly out of the house. Although I was not a Christian, I believed that on that night a Greater Power intercepted my execution.

While I got involved in gangster life with the purpose of taking out the two men who murdered my aunt, I ended up involved in so much more. Sin, or evil, has no limit to where it will take you. One may enter a gang with a plan of doing only one or two things; but the allurements and attractions of gang life can quickly lead one down a path of no return. The longer one practices evil, the more one's conscience is deadened by that lifestyle.

I know you may be wondering: Did I ever find the men who caused my family and me so much pain through the death of my aunt? Did I ever complete my mission of revenge?

# Chapter 4

## Gangster Life Inside of School

I started high school in September 2005. I spend two
years in seventh grade, since I was younger than most of the
students in my class, and also due to my gang involvement
which made my school work suffer. At that time, Old Harbour
High School, in St. Catherine Jamaica, operated under the shift
system – Grades 7 to 9 on the lower (junior), shift, and Grades
9 to 13 on the upper (senior) shift. Mr. Selvin Green was the
principal; Miss Dorman was the vice principal on the lower
shift; and Mr. Linton Weir was the vice principal on the upper
shift.

While in seventh grade, I created a junior gangster crew
among the young men at school. I taught these young men
how to handle a firearm as I was preparing for war to eliminate
my aunt's killers. As the junior "Don," I had the lower shift

## Gangster Life Inside of School

under strict management. When the bell rang signaling the resumption of classes, the boys and girls in the school corridors had to immediately find their classrooms. In addition, whenever some teachers encountered particularly troublesome classes or students, they would call for me to come and talk with them. I also carried a belt to administer corporal punishment. Upon entering one of these troubled classes, I would firmly announce, "Students, I want no talking in this class." If a boy or girl disobeyed my strict command, my belt and I would be waiting for them at the end of the class period.

After my aunt's death, all love evaporated from my heart and I was consumed by thoughts of anger, vengeance, and wrath. I would actively engage in fist, knife, and stone fights on a regular basis, both on and off the school campus. Many times my altercations blocked the school road, requiring the police to be called and get involved. As a result, week after week I was suspended for my behavior, which meant I was mandated to stay off the school grounds. Some of the parents found my place of residence and stopped by to complain to my mother about my fighting.

On some occasions my fighting episodes resulted in doctor bill after doctor bill that my mother had to pay due to injuries sustained by other students. My fighting episodes continued from 2006 to 2009. Attempts were made by the school guidance counselors, Mr. Basil Jackson and Mrs. Scully, and some teachers to understand what was happening with me.

As a track and field athlete, I participated at various track events. In April 2009, I accompanied the athletes representing my school at the Boys and Girls Championship; a national sporting event in Jamaica where high Schools compete for a national title and trophy. While there, I had a serious altercation with a fellow schoolmate that left him with severe back injuries. His parents vehemently insisted that I be expelled from school. My mother was called to a meeting in which she was told, "We can no longer tolerate Billy Mirander in Old Harbour High School."

"Where am I going to send my son," my mother responded, in great distress, to Vice Principal Mrs. Green. "With his record, no school will take him."

With a sad, pained countenance my mother pleaded for mercy. I was just a few short months away from my 16$^{th}$ birthday. Would I make it to 10th grade?

# Chapter 5

## Demons and Satanic Rituals

While engaged in gang activities in and out of school, my life took another drastic turn. As I dove deeper into gangster life, I was advised that in order to survive I would need forces of darkness to cover me. That's when I was introduced to satanic rituals and practices.

The devil has many agents and organizations through which he works, and I was made aware of a few of these. First, there was the Blood Sacrifice Organization in which animals or a person's hand are slit open, allowing the blood to flow into a container, and offered as a blood sacrifice as part of a satanic ritual. The room where these sacrifices took place had an altar and the Star of David engraved on the plates that were used.

Several years after my conversion, I mentioned those satanic ritual altars when sharing my testimony. In an article, which appeared in the *Jamaican Gleaner* on January 29, 2018,

# Demons and Satanic Rituals

the then National Security Minister, Robert Montague, told the House of Representatives, "We [Jamaican Security Forces] have discovered a most disturbing trend of which you must be made aware. We have been discovering altars to facilitate devil worship in many places where raids have been conducted by the security forces. This is a most dangerous trend, and the clergy is also disturbed by it. The savagery, the brutality and horrific nature of some crimes point to sacrifices to these evil forces."

Second, I was introduced to a group of men who engaged in a vicious series of activities called the "Gangster Take Out Gangster." Members of this group are among the most notorious gangsters. They would schedule a certain number of individuals to be eliminated on a weekly basis. Additionally, they would terminate gangsters who were no longer responding to commands and instructions given to them, or gangsters who wanted to leave the practices of the group.

# Demons and Satanic Rituals

Third, I was introduced to the Spiritism Churches. It's imperative for me to share that not every building with a cross on it means that they worship Jesus. The demonic church that I started attending met four times per week; morning and evening services every Sunday, and a service each Wednesday and Friday nights. Some of the rituals I engaged in were supposed to afford us special protection as gangsters from our enemies.

During one ritual, the Priest would instruct us to go into the bathroom and remove all of our clothes. He would pour a liquid in a bath of water, and spin the water around until it became black. He would apply the black water to our bodies, along with another ointment that was sprayed on us. After completing this ritual, he would summon a host of demons to stand with, and in, me. This gave me superhuman strength, allowing me to lift items and individuals effortlessly even though I was very slender at the time. As part of another ritual,

# Demons and Satanic Rituals

I had to slit my own hands and taste my blood to interact with, and see the manifestation of, demonic forces.

Some members of these demonic churches wore a ring; others did not. Whenever enemies would come near us, the ring would become very hot; for those who didn't wear one, our internal demons would become agitated and cause discomfort, indicating that danger was near and that it was time to move to a different location.

I thought nothing could be darker than the gang life. I realized how wrong I was, once I ventured into the demonic realm.

# Chapter Six

## My Mother's Prayer and Tears

Imagine having a 14 or 15 year old child who does not come home until 4:00 or 5:00 in the morning. Because I was patrolling the gang turf from 9 p.m. to 5 a.m., that's when I'd return home to get ready for school which began at 7 a.m. Imagine having to pay doctor bill after doctor bill for injuries caused by your child to other students.

That was my mother's world for over three years, while I was walking down the path of no return. I was so deep into the gang lifestyle, that there seemed to be no hope for my life. It reached a stage where everyone in my family turned their backs on me, except for my mother. When I came home each morning, my mother's pillow was wet with the tears she shed every night while calling on God's deliverance for me. She would not go to sleep until I came home. Most nights it appeared that my mother would wait until I came in the house

# My Mother's Prayer and Tears

to begin praying so that I could hear her. She would pray and cry, but nothing seemed to be happening. Still, she kept on praying and crying out to God for me. The words written by Gordon Jenkins, "Tears are a language God understands," aptly describes this experience.

My mother was counseled to poison my food, kill me in my sleep, or send me to Fumitory School – a Jamaican phrase for juvenile home. By that time, I had a different stepfather. He gave my mother an ultimatum to either put me out of his house, or leave with me. She readily chose to leave instead of turning her back on me. For parents – and specifically for mothers – who have wayward children that you've been praying for and nothing seems to be happening, I want to challenge you to never give up. Even in the darkest hours, when a lifestyle transformation or conversion seems impossible, don't give up on your children.

## My Mother's Prayer and Tears

On Page 61 of the book, *Prayer*, by Christian author Ellen G. White, is one of the most powerful statements I've read on prayer. She says, "Prayer and faith will do what no power on earth can ever do or ever accomplish."

Even though there appeared to be no visible changes as my mother prayed for me, behind the scenes the angels of God and the Holy Spirit were beginning their work in my life.

## Chapter 7

## First Revelations of God and the Bible

After the fallout between my stepfather and me, I was no longer living in the house with the rest of my siblings. I was staying at one of his other houses. My greatest idol during this period of my life was a popular dancehall artist, whom God recognized as the only person who could get my attention.

One day my idol said something to me like, "With all you've done, with all the horrific events you've been through – gang bangs and shootouts – you've never been shot. Do you know there is a God in heaven protecting you?" Then, he encouraged me to pray and read the Bible; so I searched the house and found one.

Each morning, I had to smoke before I could eat or do any work. With the Bible in hand, I prepared my marijuana spliff, or cigarette. With each verse I read, I took a puff. I read

# First Revelations of God and the Bible

the book of Psalms and went unto the book of Proverbs. I was

amazed at what I found in the Bible. I began to spend hours

reading the Bible daily while smoking my joints.

At this time, September 2009, I was about to be

expelled from school. However, I was given a final opportunity

by the former Vice Principal, now newly appointed Principal,

Mr. Linton Weir, to get myself together. Mr. Weir was the best

principal to ever lead Old Harbour High School. He told me

that he was aware that I was the Don for my shift, but he made

it crystal clear that he was the leader of the school. He evoked a

Jamaican phrase that says, "Two bull can't reign in one pen."

After my first Bible study, I got to school and called

together my gang troops to share with them what I was

learning from the Bible. I had not been exposed to so much

wisdom before. I quoted scriptures to them: "The fear of the

Lord is the beginning of wisdom." Proverbs 9:10, KJV. "The

fear of the Lord is to hate evil." Proverbs 8:13, KJV. "The

curse of the Lord is in the house of the wicked." Proverbs 3:33, KJV. I also told them that if they hurt somebody who had caused hurt to an innocent person, that was not wickedness; they were doing God's service. But if they hurt somebody who was an innocent person, that was wickedness; so do not practice wickedness. At that time, I didn't know any better. As Acts 17:30 says, in times of ignorance, God winks at us.     At the end of the session I said, "Let us pray."

The majority of my troops ran outside, declaring that they did not want me to pray down demons on them. One of the young ladies called me aside and looked at me as though I was crazy.

"Billy are you alright? Are you taking something?" she asked.

"No," I responded. I told her I was learning some things from the Bible that I thought could help me govern our gangster life. I told her that as I learned more I would share it.

# First Revelations of God and the Bible

Some of the others said that they wouldn't be coming back to any Bible sessions, and I assured them that if they refused to come, I would execute strong disciplinary measures.

Now that I had started reading the Bible, I wanted to know personally if God existed right then, or was He just a God who operated in biblical times. I had read the story of God answering Elijah's prayer in the book of Kings, bringing a dead young man back to life, and I was deeply moved. So, I prayed about some specific things, challenging God to answer my prayer if He was the God of Elijah and the God of the Bible. When He did, I was convinced – beyond the shadow of a doubt – that God is real, and I wanted to follow Him. However, it was hard to make that decision, because I still had my gangster enemies who wanted to kill me; and I was still obligated to the demonic rituals that I had to attend, or face death.

# Chapter 8

## The Three Great Miracles that Got My Attention

At this point, I had grown to believe in God and I knew He answered prayer. Now that I'd developed an interest in spiritual things, God began to reveal even more of Himself to me through some unforgettable life experiences that really got my attention.

One of the first experiences was a toothache. I felt such intense pain that I didn't just cry – I bawled. My mother even said to me, "How comes you're a gangster, and you're crying?" We tried over-the-counter pain relievers, but the pain did not stop. My mother took me to see a doctor, yet the pain did not stop. She even took me to the hospital for a special injection that's supposed to kill intense pain; still, the pain did not stop. Instead, it seemed like the pain turned up, getting more intense.

# The Three Great Miracles that Got My Attention

My frustration was at its peak and I could not take it any longer. I cried out in agony, "God, please stop the pain, I can't bear it any longer!" Immediately the pain paused. Then I said, "God, You're the one really causing this pain." I decided that I would stay up the entire night and read the Bible and pray because I did not want the pain to come back. At that time, I didn't know better, so once again God winked at my ignorance.

I wanted to follow God; but I still had my gangster enemies who wanted to kill me and my obligations to the Demonic Church. I also had not forgotten about my vow to exact revenge for my aunt's killers. Living for God was not fitting into my plans right then; but God was working His own plan.

As the school Don, it was an unspoken rule that I had the first relationship with any new girl who came to the school. During the spring semester of my 10th grade year a new girl enrolled. At first, I didn't realize that she was new since I was

# The Three Great Miracles that Got My Attention

keeping a low profile based on my talk with Mr. Weir. Once I did, I told her of the policy but she firmly refused my advances. I let her know that the consequence for shutting me down was that she wouldn't receive attention from any young men in the school. And I made sure that she didn't. I told the young men that if any of them called her or so much as even looked at her, I would gouge their eyes out.

After two weeks, she came to me complaining that none of the young men in the school paid her any attention.

"What did you do to them?" she asked me.

I didn't bother to answer her question. I told her that if she complied with the policy, all would be well. She threatened to tell her gangster brother and let him deal with me. I promptly told her that I feared no one, and outright forgot about her threat.

Shortly after that encounter, my then girlfriend asked me to walk her to a taxi stand, so I did. When I was about to go, she held on to me and asked me to stay with her a little longer. Against my better judgement, I stayed. When the taxi arrived, she kissed me, got into the taxi and waved goodbye. As soon as I turned to leave, I saw about 30 men – along with the new girl from school – heading in my direction. As they got closer, she stated to her brother, "He is Billy."

Usually I always have a firearm or some weapon on me to defend myself, but this time I had nothing. I was upset with myself for not having anything for protection. The group of men approaching me held various weapons; knives, ice picks, and other harmful instruments. I was standing close to a jerk chicken street vendor who called out to the men. "Please, please, don't kill him right here. Please go somewhere else." The vendor knew that if they killed me in front of his food stand, nobody would ever come back and buy anything from him.

One of the men grabbed me by my shirt collar and

dragged me away. They began punching me, blow after blow. I saw the knife coming directly towards my eyes, and other parts of my body. I was convinced that I was finally going to die. I thought, "There's no way I will get out of this alive." The beating continued for about 10-15 minutes. Just then, a Don from another area came on the scene.

"Let him go," he said. "And nobody else touch him."

At this command, all the men stopped in their tracks and walked away. After they left, I started to make my way home. I took off my shirt, assuming that the punches and sharp weapons hitting me had left me bloody. But to my amazement, there was no blood; there wasn't even bruising or pain on any part of my body. When I got home I locked myself into the bathroom, and began talking with God. "God, I am praying to You and these men aren't; yet You let them almost kill me!" I was determined to pay those men back for what they did to me. But I was also determined to sit in that bathroom until God told me why He allowed them to attack me.

After spending hours on my knees, a strong wind came into the bathroom. The wind was so strong that it lifted the shower curtain up to the point that the iron curtain rod smashed into the bathroom mirror, breaking it. Then I heard a voice saying, "I want you to understand that I am the Greatest Protector."

Through that experience I realized that a firearm couldn't offer me true protection, so I decided right then not to carry one anymore. I hadn't had one when I needed it the most, and God had just told me it wouldn't protect me anyway. I felt that this decision, though, would make me easy prey for my enemies.

Once again, I felt a strong urge to follow God, but I didn't see how I could really do that. The threat of death from abandoning the demonic rituals I engaged in stood in the way.

Just before school closed for the summer, it was time

# The Three Great Miracles that Got My Attention

for the prefects – class monitors – to be chosen. Mr. Stewart, one of the 11<sup>th</sup> grade supervisors, along with Mr. Jeffrey Douglas, one of the 10<sup>th</sup> grade supervisors, met with a few administrators to choose prefects for the next school year. In an unheard of decision, they recommended that the number one "bad" girl and the number one "bad" boy – me – be appointed to the Prefect Body. I was stunned!

At Old Harbour High School, usually each year's Prefect Body identified a project to implement at the end of their year of service. Since I was selected to serve for the upcoming school year, the head prefect, Dwayne Lewis – a Seventh-day Adventist (SDA) Christian young man – asked me if I could assist him with the project they had chosen. I was reluctant to help, but agreed to do it.

The next day I showed up at the school even though summer break had officially started. The prefects were actively engaged in a landscaping project. Dwayne asked me to assist them just for five minutes. After pondering his request, I agreed. Before I knew it, my five minutes turned into an hour, then the entire day, and – surprisingly – the entire week. This caused me to miss the demonic ritual services I usually attended. When Saturday came, we didn't have to work because Dwayne, as an SDA, didn't work on Saturday. Exhausted from the week, I slept all that day.

I had actually begun to enjoy working on the project, so I went back the following week. Again, I missed another week of the demonic ritual services. Remember, when I joined the Demonic Church I was told that if I missed any of the meetings I would be killed. After missing two weeks, my family and I received numerous threats saying that if I didn't return, I'd be killed. But I didn't go back. Two weeks turned into three weeks, and before long, I'd been absent for over a month. By this time I had crossed the line, and several strange things started happening; my clothes went missing, and money went missing. The Church sent me one last warning; either return or end up a dead man.

As the new school year loomed, I needed to get a new school uniform. As an incoming prefect, I needed the white shirts that prefects wore to distinguish themselves from the other students. In August 2010, one month before school resumed, there was no money available to purchase my school uniform. Principal Weir called me and asked if I needed assistance with back-to-school expenses. When I responded yes, he offered to give me $JA10,000 (the equivalent of $80 US dollars) for the work I'd done with the prefects, even though I had done it as a volunteer. I gratefully accepted. His help allowed me to purchase two white shirts and two pairs of khaki pants, along with school shoes and a school bag.

By this time, all of my strong feelings for revenge against my aunt's killers and the men who'd beat me up were waning as my spiritual convictions grew stronger. But in the

## The Three Great Miracles that Got My Attention

back of my mind, I knew my gangster enemies would be

coming after me.

# Chapter 9

## Sabbath Revelation & Official Visit to SDA Church

A few evenings after receiving the threats from the Demonic Church, I was at home when a terrible headache rocked my world. It was accompanied by a heaviness that engulfed me, and spasms of breathlessness. With the last breath I could muster I cried out, "God, are you going to let me die like this? If you give me one more chance, I will stop smoking and I will serve You." Immediately, the pain stopped. Then I vomited. I'd made the decision to serve God in the face of the full knowledge that my gangster enemies and the demons would return to kill me.

The next day I was sitting on the couch at my stepfather's house, contemplating about which church to attend now that I'd decided to follow the Lord. I felt confused because there were so many denominations. I started reading the Bible to get answers, and I fell asleep with that question on my mind. I was jolted awake by a crashing sound, like a car crash. I heard a voice say, "Take up your Bible and go to the extreme side of the house." I picked up my Bible, went outside and started to the other side of the house.

On the way, I passed my mother who was standing alone at the back fence, putting out some clothes on the line. As I sat outside on the bathroom pit, I opened up my Bible to a text about the seventh day Sabbath. I thought to myself, "Who do I know that attends a Sabbath-keeping church?" Just then the sunlight became intensely bright, and I saw a figure of a man who I recognized as Derek Thompson, the gardener who usually cut my mother's lawn. As I gazed at Derek I asked, "God, does he go to a Sabbath church?"

A voice responded, "Yes, ask him."

A feeling of sheer shock overwhelmed me and I felt compelled to ask my mother for Derek's number. I immediately got up and headed in her direction. When I got to where my mother stood, my jaw dropped open. Standing there talking to my mother was Derek Thompson. I hastily said, "Mommy, please excuse me, Derek, which church do you go to"?

Derek responded, "I attend the Berea Seventh-day Adventist Church." He went on to share with me that they met in the auditorium of the Old Harbour Primary School. He told me they had Sabbath School and Divine Hour services in the morning, and lunch and Bible class in the afternoon.

"Well, I'm coming to church this Saturday," I announced.

Derek looked shocked. My mother was overjoyed. It was only Tuesday, but my mother pressed my clothes, cleaned my shoes, and bought my favorite meal from KFC and put it in the fridge for me to have for Sabbath lunch. She told the entire

# Sabbath Revelation & Official Visit to SDA Church

community that I was going to church on Saturday, and to pray for me.

To this day, that week is etched in my mind. During that week, my mother gave me breakfast in bed, dinner in bed, and warned my siblings not give me any trouble because she didn't want me to change my mind. The week speed by quickly, and when Saturday came, I made my first official visit to the Berea SDA Church. The Divine Service was not so interesting to me; but the Bible class was a different story. At that point, I hungered for biblical teaching rather than preaching. At times, there are some things that teaching will give you that preaching won't.

At the afternoon Bible class, Elder Glenn Heaven was conducting a Revelation Seminar. That day his focus was on the Investigative Judgement. He pointed out text after text that clearly illustrated that the judgment was going on now, and that when Jesus returns, every case would've already been decided.

54

When that bit of information registered on my frontal lobe, every organ in my body felt like it was starting to break down. What a startling revelation!

The Demonic Church had taught me that when Christ returns, He would line us up and – even if we did something wrong while He was in mid-air – by the time Christ reached the earth, we could quickly ask for forgiveness and He would forgive us and permit us to go to heaven. When light comes, darkness must go. I instantly raised my hand and asked, "Elder, please pray for me," which he did immediately.

During the next week, every evening – at the same time – all of my past horrific deeds flashed before me, and a voice said, "This is your final opportunity to accept Me." I went to church the next Sabbath and I learned about some of the fundamental beliefs of the SDA church. I asked so many questions, for which I received biblical answers.

"How can I become a member of this church?" I asked Elder Heaven.

He said that I would need to speak with the Pastor.

I said, "Elder, tell the Pastor that I'm ready to be baptized, right now." I was deeply convicted of the Bible truths I was hearing.

# Chapter 10

## Church and School Opposition

In August 2010, Pastor Johnathan Miller was the Senior Pastor, and Pastor Dorian Kelly, was the Junior Pastor at the Berea SDA Church. An appointment was made for me to speak with Pastor Kelly and the Bible Worker, Elder Alex Edgar, about being baptized. As Elder Edgar prepared to speak with me to ensure that I was prepared for baptism, he was cautioned by members of the church, who were also teachers at my school, about going to meet with a "gangster," as they were aware of my behavior. As a faithful minister of Christ, Elder Edgar ignored the protests and came to prepare me for baptism. He understood that gangsters needed Jesus too.

I was informed that the next baptismal service was scheduled for Sunday, September 12, 2010. However, when my name was presented to the church board as a baptismal candidate, most of the members were not in favour of me

joining the church as a member because of my past.

Nevertheless, Pastor Kelly and Elders Edgar and Heaven

persisted for my baptism.

Prior to Old Harbour High School's 2010-2011

academic year, I had to attend a seminar for incoming prefects,

conducted under the leadership of the Prefect Body

Coordinator, Mr. Andre Hinds. It was customary that during

the seminar, the Prefect Body would choose one student to

serve as the Inspector Coordinator, who was responsible for

discipline and dress code inspection. In Jamaica, because

students wear school uniforms, specific standards govern the

length and width of both the male and female uniforms. The

Inspector Coordinator ensured that students complied with

these standards. The Prefect Body, not knowing the changes

that had taken place in my heart during the summer, voted for me to serve as the Inspector Coordinator of the male students.

In September, on the first day of school, I was at my post of duty at the gate, inspecting each male's uniform. My female counterpart inspected the girls' uniforms. As I was doing my job, a teacher drove up, rolled down the car window and exclaimed, "Jesus, Billy in a white shirt!" This was repeated by several other teachers who were outraged by my selection as a prefect. They immediately went to Principal Weir and said, "Mr. Weir, are you crazy? How can Billy be serving as a prefect?"

Without giving Mr. Weir the opportunity to answer, another teacher exclaimed, "What is this school going to? Billy is a prefect!"

"Colleagues," Mr. Weir responded, "I see something great in this young man."

## Church and School Opposition

"Then you must be blind, Mr. Weir," another teacher butted in. Despite Mr. Weir's appeals, the disgruntled teachers refused to be won over. In the meantime, I was hiding in a classroom, mortified by everyone calling the Lord's name down on me. It is never a welcoming position to be in to have Jamaicans call down Jesus' name on you. I was so distressed, I decided to leave school and go home.

When I got home I flatly told my mother that I was not going back to school, and quickly relayed the day's events to her. She comforted me, and encouraged me to pray and to go back to school the next day, which I did. During general devotion – where all the students, teachers, and administrators come together to start the school day with worship – Mrs. Bell Jackson, the head of the Agriculture Department, was leading out, assisted by two prefects, Lasha Longmore and Aneka Smikle. Mrs Jackson announced to the school that we would

## Church and School Opposition

sing a prayer chorus, "Trust in the Lord," after which I'd pray. As I approached the lectern, the students stared at me. Some refused to close their eyes and put both hands on their hips, in a matter- of- fact manner. Others rolled and cut their eyes at me. Even some of the teachers commented that my praying would call down a curse on the school.

I was so nervous, that my hands shook as I held the microphone. Then I closed my eyes to blot out all the negative vibrations, and I prayed. When I ended with, "Amen," and opened my eyes, the entire school looked amazed. It was such an unexpected, surreal moment. Here I was, a guy that everyone knew as a "trouble maker and gangster," who now stood before them having prayed. I appeared to be completely transformed. "What on earth has happened to Billy?" was the talk of the school that entire day.

# Chapter 11

## Demonic Attack & the Name of the Lord

On Thursday of that week while on the playground after school, I was surrounded by a dense blackness. I literally felt a hand close around my throat, suffocating me, while at the same time feeling like I was being beaten all over my body. In the distance, I saw my classmates and tried to call for help; but I couldn't hear my voice – as though no sound came out. Once again I was certain that the curtains were closing on my life. This was it!

Just then, a Bible text I had learned flashed through my mind. "The name of the LORD is a strong tower: the righteous runneth into it, and is safe." Proverbs 18:10, KJV. I called out the name of Jesus two times. After the third time I called out, 'Jesus,' I heard the sound of breaking glass. I was set free! Every demon was dispelled.

There is power, victory and deliverance in the name of Jesus. Whenever a sincere soul calls upon the name of the

## Demonic Attack & the Name of the Lord

Lord, God will intervene. God took care of the demons; however, my gangster enemies were still a threat.

# Chapter 12

## Night of Baptism and the Power of the Grace of God

Although faced with opposition about my baptism, I presented myself on Sunday, September 12, 2010 at the Old Harbour SDA Church to be baptized. Even though we were using that church for baptism, my membership would belong at the Berea SDA Church.

Nine months prior to that day, God had begun revealing Himself to me, convicting me to follow Jesus all the way. On baptism day, a large contingent of community residents, students and teachers from my high school, and church members came to the service. As I stood at the altar preparing to take the vows to follow Jesus all the way, I looked toward the side door. There stood my gangster enemies. One of them pulled up his shirt to show me his gun and signalled that they were waiting outside to blow me away. I remained calm so as not to alert the congregation who didn't see what was happening outside.

Pastor Dorian Kelly administered the baptismal vows.

After taking the vows, I went into the bathroom to change into my white baptismal robe. There, on the floor, I knelt down and prayed, "Lord Jesus, please forgive me of all the things that I have done. If You have a plan for my life, save me from the hands of my enemies. But if I die tonight, let it be well with my soul." Pastor Johnathan Miller baptized me, along with two other ladies, in the name of the Father, Son, and Holy Ghost. It was one month before my 17$^{th}$ birthday. My soul was overjoyed.

Just before I left the church grounds, my gangster enemies who were waiting outside, approached me.

"Billy, you really changed?" they asked.

"Yes, I have," I responded.

They looked at me, then said, "We also want to

experience the grace of God in our lives as well. Pray for us," they beseeched me.

Some of my enemies were so moved by my commitment to follow Jesus, that not long after my baptism they, too, accepted Jesus as Lord. The Bible is real! "When a man's ways please the Lord, He makes even his enemies to be at peace with him," says Proverbs 16:7, KJV. In addition, almost my entire family became members of the SDA church, after seeing what God had done in my life.

That same year I was appointed as the Deputy Head Boy at Old Harbour High School. Teachers, school mates, and those in the community asked me time and time again, "Billy, what has really happened to you?" Humbly I responded that I found out there is POWER in the blood of Jesus. As the song says, His blood reaches to lowest valley, and it soars to the highest mountain. That blood will never, ever lose its power (A. Crouch, *The Blood Will Never Lose Its Power*).

# Night of Baptism & the Power of the Grace of God

For almost one year after my conversion, I visited the families and individuals who were affected by my negative actions and asked their forgiveness, which they granted me. I know what it feels like to be freed. John 8:36, says it best: Whom the Son sets free, is free indeed.

Whoever you are today, I want you to know that the vilest offender who truly believes, in that very moment, from Jesus a pardon receives (F. Crosby, *To God Be the Glory*).

A few years after my conversion, I had just completed my first Evangelistic Tent Crusade in Portmore, St. Catherine, Jamaica when, after all this time, I saw my aunt's children's father. Since her murder, I had made numerous attempts to find him in my quest for revenge, yet all my attempts proved futile. Now, his back was turned to me, and I was so close to him that I placed my hand on his shoulder. He spun around and our eyes locked. He tried run away because he knew I'd been searching for him for a long time to avenge my aunt's death.

## Night of Baptism & the Power of the Grace of God

I held him firmly and said, "You don't have to run anymore, because, I've met Jesus and He's brought about a great change in me." Before he departed, I encouraged him to put his trust in God.

In the world today, so many individuals are battling thoughts of unforgiveness and revenge because of the hurt and pain that someone, somewhere, has caused you or your family. Dear reader, I want to personally encourage you to give it to the Lord. The thoughts of revenge and unforgiveness that bound me after my aunt's murder were broken by the grace of God. Because of God's Grace which forgave me, I, in turn, could forgive my aunt's murderers for the pain and hurt they caused my family and me.

Today, Jesus wants to give you a wonderful exchange. He desires to give you "beauty for ashes, the oil of joy for mourning, the garment of praise for the spirit of heaviness." Isaiah 61:3, KJV.

# Chapter 13

## Becoming an Evangelist & Prayer Ministry Leader

After my conversion, Elders Dwight Brown and Trevor McClore, elders at the Berea SDA Church, continued to instruct me and nurture my faith, making sure that I clearly understood the church doctrines. I received the sincere milk of the Word, enabling me to grow in my walk with the Lord. They also gave me opportunities to participate in the services at Berea SDA church.

Not long after, Pastor Glendon Caballero, a minister of the Gospel who, at that time was affiliated with the Central Jamaica Conference of SDA, came to preach at Berea, my home church. We were introduced, and I shared with him my testimony. He took me under his wings, teaching me the basic principles of serving as a Bible worker while also giving me field experience. He gave me the first opportunity to preach

# Becoming an Evangelist & Prayer Ministry Leader

God's Word during the Divine Service, the main worship service convened each Sabbath during which the main highlight is a sermon from the Word of God.

God used Pastor Caballero to play a vital role in my ministry development. He introduced me to numerous local pastors, and the Jamaican conference and union leaders. He briefly shared my experiences with them and they, in turn, invited me to their respective churches to preach God's Word and share my life testimony.

Since giving my life to Jesus and joining the SDA church in 2010, I've preached in over 150 churches, in Jamaica and five countries including the United States of America. I've preached in several states in the U.S., proclaiming the undisputable fact that Jesus saves. I've served as a Bible worker and evangelist in several evangelistic programs, including special Sabbath celebrations, Week of Prayer services, revivals, and crusades. By the working of God's Holy

Spirit, over 300 precious souls have surrendered to Jesus by way of baptism into the SDA church, through my evangelistic ministry.

I've been featured on television, on radio, and in newspaper articles, sharing my experiences to inspire others. I've been a featured motivational speaker at graduation ceremonies and other youth forums, including the Governor General Program of Excellence (GGPE), National Youth Consultative Conference, and the I Believe Initiative (IBI), where I was blessed to impact the lives of hundreds of young people representing the 14 parishes in Jamaica.

From very early in my Christian walk, I came to understand that one of the principal keys to success in the Christian pathway is prayer. "Prayer is the breath of the soul. It is the secret of spiritual power. No other means of grace can be substituted, and the health of the soul be preserved" (E.G. White from *Prayer*, p. 84). I've seen God manifest His power so many times in my life, there is no shadow of doubt in my mind that God not only hears, but answers prayer.

From time to time, I would call my church brothers and sisters and pray with them over the phone as a means of encouraging them. One day the thought came to me to gather together several of my prayer partners on one conference call prayer session. The first time I did it, five people were connected on the call. We prayed together and encouraged each other. From that point, we started praying at set times each morning and evening. Some joined in on the morning session, and others joined in each evening. That's how "Jesus is the Way Prayer Ministry" was born.

I shared my desire to establish the prayer ministry as an official ministry, with Pastor Dudley Mullings, a minister of the Gospel in the Central Jamaica Conference of SDAs. He guided me in preparing a constitution and bylaws to regulate the operations of the Prayer Ministry. The ministry grew to comprise members from the various conferences within the Jamaica Union. Both the Union Prayer Ministry Coordinator and the President of the Central Jamaica Conference of SDA endorsed the ministry. Pastor Robert Wright, Director of the Ellen G. White Research Centre at Northern Caribbean University, currently serves as the Advisor to the Prayer Ministry.

The ministry has impacted hundreds of souls through our quarterly prayer conventions, prayer walks, and community outreach endeavours. We've seen conversion breakthroughs and answered prayers through our Telephone Prayer-line sessions. Jeremiah 33:3 reminds us that when we call, God has promised to answer and show us great and mighty things.

# Chapter 14

## Marriage and Academic Pursuit

In January 2014, I enrolled at Northern Caribbean University where I was accepted to pursue a Bachelor of Arts in Business Administration with an Accounting emphasis. After the first semester, due to my passion for teaching and a desire to impact students at the secondary level – based on my own experiences – I changed my major to a Bachelor of Arts in Teacher Education with an emphasis in Business.

During my first semester, I participated in an evangelistic campaign at Dunsinane Seventh-day Adventist Church. Dr. Newton Cleghorne, the then Dean of the School of Religion & Theology at Northern Caribbean University who I'd met through the Prayer Ministry, heard me share the Word of God and my personal testimony. Afterwards, he told me about a young lady, Abigail Foster, who he believed would complement my ministry well. That was exactly what the

## Marriage and Academic Pursuit

Prayer Ministry members and I had been praying about for over two years – that God would send me a suitable wife who would complement and support my ministry.

During school registration at the Business Office, I met Abigail, who was working in that a division of the University. I thought she was very beautiful, and I admired her greatly. She was an intelligent, God-fearing woman who provided excellent customer service. I felt she was just the right type of person I needed as a life partner, and I wanted her to be my wife. However, getting her to agree to marry me was no easy task. It was through much prayer, and persistence over two years of courtship, that this virtuous woman finally became my wife on December 18, 2016. I got married to the "one whom my soul loves." Song of Solomon 3:4, KJV.

Abigail has significantly impacted my ministry. She serves as the secretary for the prayer and evangelistic ministries. She manages my schedule and appointments, designs the promotional flyers for ministry events, and arranges my travel. She provides me invaluable emotional and spiritual support, and so much more to assist me in fulfilling my God-appointed mission.

In October of 2017, I conducted a one-week revival at the Mount Calvary SDA Church in Tampa, Florida. God used me to call 13 precious souls into a saving relationship with Jesus. During the revival I stayed with Elder Moses Brown, a chaplain at Florida Hospital and an elder at the Mount Calvary SDA Church. He, along with Pastor Curtis Crider, the Senior Pastor of Mount Calvary, each spoke to me separately about seriously considering going into ministry full time. This is something that several pastors had already encouraged me to do. But this time, there was something more compelling about Elder Brown and Pastor Crider's appeal.

I made their suggestion a matter of prayer and deep contemplation. Finally, I was convicted that full-time ministry was God's will for my life. When I yielded my will to the Divine will, I found peace. As I considered where to pursue my ministerial studies, I thought about counsel I had received,

and my own personal experience preaching in other countries.

In light of Revelation 14:7-8 which calls us to reach people

from every tribe, tongue, and people, I felt that obtaining a

multicultural experience would better equip me to become a

more effective instrument in God's hands. Thus, I opted for

schooling outside of Jamaica.

I applied to Oakwood University in November 2017.

God worked in such a remarkable way that by January 2018,

Abigail and I were in Huntsville, Alabama for me to begin my

program of study. I am presently pursuing a Bachelor of Arts in

Ministerial Theology with a minor in Biblical Languages.

On June 16, 2018 at 8:56 p.m., we became the proud

parents of a beautiful, baby girl, Isabella Rachel Mirander.

Borrowing the words made popular by Gospel singing artist,

Hezekiah Walker – as they aptly describe my experience – I

can't help but give God the glory, went I think about my story.

## Marriage and Academic Pursuit

As my journey unfolds day by day, I live with this settled assurance; "I have nothing to fear for the future, except as I shall forget the way the Lord has led me, and His teaching in my past history" (E.G. White from *Life Sketches*, p. 196).

# Chapter 15

## Final Message and Heart Appeal

Dear Reader: Distance, and time zones may separate us, but the human experience transcends, nation, tribes, and tongues. I wish to share these parting heart-to-heart counsels with you, based on my own life's journey.

I know what it feels like to be rejected. I know what it feels like to wish that you could start your life over again, I know what it feels like to struggle with addictions that seem too hard to break. I thought marijuana, sex, and gambling were too powerful to stop, demon possession too binding, and blood-thirsty enemies too hardhearted. But then I met Jesus. He is more powerful than any drugs, stronger than anything or anyone binding you, and the best protector. Even the hardest gangster mind is like the wave of the sea with Him; He can turn it wither He will, according to Proverbs 21:1.

As one who has been marked for death more times than

# Final Message and Heart Appeal

I can count, I want you to know that no matter how deep in sin you are, there is still hope. There is power in the blood of Jesus. He can still change your heart, change your life, and change your circumstances. Hebrews 7: 25, KJV says, "He is able also to save them to the uttermost that come unto God by him, seeing he ever liveth to make intercession for them."

What Jesus did on Calvary is for *you*, and it is also for me. "He was wounded for our transgressions, He was bruised for our iniquities, the chastisement of our peace was upon Him, and with His stripes, we are healed." Isaiah 53: 5, KJV. Jesus has taken the punishment for every soul, no matter how fallen your condition. For this reason, He can ransom your soul if you will choose to accept His offer of forgiveness, and His standard of righteousness.

Personally, I want to assure you that the best decision that you could ever make in this life is to choose Jesus as Lord of your life. Once you've made that decision and surrendered

# Final Message and Heart Appeal

your life to Him in baptism, the walk has only just begun. To get to know someone, it's imperative to talk with that person. That's why as a Christian, prayer must become the connecting link between your soul and God. He will never, ever get tired of hearing from you. When you take the time to talk with God, He will not only listen to your heart's cry, but He will also answer your prayer.

For any relationship to be healthy, one person cannot do all the talking because that would be a monologue, not a dialogue. The same is true of your relationship with Jesus. He speaks to us through His Word. The Scriptures are the voice of God to our souls. We can hear Him speak to us, just as any earthly friend, if we are willing to set aside special times – especially in the mornings – for the opportunity to sit at the feet of Jesus. "When every other voice is hushed, and in quietness we wait before him, the silence of the soul makes more distinct the voice of God" (E.G. White from *Desire of Ages*, p. 363). In many instances when I open my Bible and read, it has not ceased to reveal to me the very counsel that matched my situation and circumstances. Have you taken time to listen to God today?

Our limbs become strong from exercise. If we fail to exercise our limbs, they become weak and frail. Similarly, if we fail to share our faith with others, our Christian experience becomes fickle and dull, and spiritual death is imminent. For this reason, after we've given our hearts to Jesus we should speak to others of His power and grace. It is for this reason, that no matter where I travel, I make it my point of duty to tell of the great things that Jesus has done for me. Man may refute the sacred scriptures, but who can argue about one's personal testimony of what Jesus has done?

Apart from spending time with Jesus, it's also good to associate with positive role models and mentors who can encourage you. In my life, Principal Weir and Pastor Caballero

## Final Message and Heart Appeal

were both men who believed in me and went out on a limb for me. They were willing to risk association with me, in spite of my past. Likewise, you will need to have some people in your corner who believe in you and are willing to let you know. It may come at a time when you don't believe in yourself.

When several teachers had counted me out, Mr. Weir counted me in. He guided me and taught me how to be a leader. Even to this day, he is forever a source of constant inspiration to me. I remember things from the session we had where he taught me about the operations of the Old Harbour High School. At that time, Principal Weir managed 2500 enrolled students, 133 teachers, 19 ancillary workers, seven administrators, three guidance counselors, three vice principals, and a Dean of Discipline. Mr. Linton Weir, I salute you as a leader extraordinaire.

When church members wrote me off, Pastor Caballero, God's man, was willing to write me up. For the lessons I

# Final Message and Heart Appeal

learned from him, the opportunities he afforded me, and the love he lavished on me, I salute you, Pastor Caballero, as a true under shepherd of the flock, and a pastor of no mean order.

Several others in my church family were a source of emotional, spiritual and financial help to me at beginning of my Christian experience: Elder Dwight Brown, Elder Trevor Mc- Clore, Sister Georgia Hamilton, Brother Carlos King, members of the Berea SDA Church in St. Catherine, Jamaica. They served as confidants that I could relate to, prayer partners that would pray with and for me, and were encouraging me to "press towards the mark of the high calling in Jesus Christ our Lord." Philippians 3:14, KJV.

The Christian pathway is not without challenges. Jesus says in John 16:33, KJV, "In the world ye shall have tribulation, but be of good cheer; I have overcome the world." 1 Peter 4:12, KJV says, "Beloved think it not strange, concerning the fiery trials that will try you; though some strange things will happen among you."

As Christians, we're going to experience some great challenges in life; but be mindful that we serve a God who is able. Our God knows how to shut the lion's mouth; He knows how to quench the heat of the fire; He knows how to part our Red Sea. The text in Isaiah 43:2 says, be assured that if you are going through the waters, He will be with you; through the rivers, they will not overflow you; through the fire, you will not be burned.

Let us not be fearful, because Christ has already won the battle on Calvary's cross. He is just a prayer away.

Made in the USA
Middletown, DE
09 March 2019